Accumulus

ETHAN PAQUIN is the author of *The Makeshift*, which was published in England in 2002 and appears in this book for the first time outside the UK. He created and has been editor of the international poetry journal *Slope* (www.slope.org) since 1999, and in 2001 founded the small press, Slope Editions. His poetry has been published throughout the US, Europe and Australia, and his criticism appears in journals including *The Boston Review, Verse, Canadian Review of Books* and *Contemporary Poetry Review*, for which he is contributing editor. A native of New Hampshire, he is Assistant Professor of Humanities at Medaille College in Buffalo, NY.

Accumulus

Ethan Paquin

SALT

PUBLISHED BY SALT PUBLISHING
PO Box 937, Great Wilbraham, Cambridge PDO CB1 5JX United Kingdom
PO Box 202, Applecross, Western Australia 6153

© Ethan Paquin, 2003

The right of Ethan Paquin to be identified as the
author of this work has been asserted by him in accordance
with Section 77 of the Copyright, Designs and Patents Act 1988.

First published 2003

Printed and bound in the United Kingdom by Lightning Source

Typeset in Swift 9.5 / 13

ISBN 1 84471 015 7 paperback

SP

1 3 5 7 9 8 6 4 2

Contents

Acknowledgments

The author gratefully acknowledges the editors of the following publications in which some of these poems first appeared, occasionally in different form:

The Makeshift

American Letters & Commentary ("Box," "Episodic"); *Arena Magazine* ("Textures of Domesticity"); *The Boston Review* ("More Like Montpelier"); *Boulevard* ("Awake, First Light"); *Canadian Review of Books* ("Rooms, Steadily Darkening"); *Conduit* ("Melancholia," "One Field"); *Forklift, Ohio* ("Diary"); *Leviathan Quarterly* ("Apogee Brevita"); *Lit* ("Bolus," "Just Before Diversion," "Not This, Mirror" from "The Mandarin," "To a Child Not Afraid of the Dark"); *Maisonneuve* ("Having Learned to Sing, I Find it Difficult"); *Meanjin* ("Wanderer"); *New American Writing* ("Sad," "Sonata"); *Overland* ("Apostasy"); *Painted Bride Quarterly* ("Laughter is X, Laughter is Y"); *Plastic* ("Two Hypotheses" from "The Mandarin"); *Quarterly West* ("Lingerings Near Southern April," "The Makeshift," "The Near-Miss Slides"); *Tooth* ("Flight Pattern," "The Use of Reinhardt"); *Untitled: A Magazine of Prose Poetry* ("Study of Three Men With Faces Painted by Francis Bacon") and *Verse* ("Terrarium, a Quincunx").

Poems also appeared online in *Bathhouse* ("Entries Fitted for Freezing Rain"), *CrossConnect* ("Interpreter," from "The Mandarin"), *Jacket* ("A Vision, Winter," "Ghazal," "Like the Song Goes, 'There's a Man With," "Terrarium, a Quincunx") and *La Petite Zine* ("Canned Cloudscape"). *Nerve* accepted "Rural Notebook" in 2001. "Reverie" appeared in the CD-rom journal *Papertiger*.

Dead July

Both ("Anteros"); *Boulevard* ("Like an Empty"); *Crowd* ("Portrait With the Entrance of Dusk . . . ," "Thunder Over Louisville"); *Ecopoetics* ("High Horizon"); *Jack Mackerel* ("Ars Cryotica"), *Leviathan Quarterly* ("Girl, Night"); *Lit* ("The Good"); *Maisonneuve* ("Having No One Else to Turn to, I Consult the Night Hour," "End/Again"); *New American Writing* ("Dark Sky and Bulb From Miles Away"); *NowCulture* ("Procession," "Wistful"); *Pequod* ("Scythe and Dory"); *Pleiades* ("When I Don't Think of This World"); *Pool* ("Mountains Falling"); *The Prague Review* ("Errata," "The Rest"); *Skein* ("Poem I've Written, It – ," "Troubled by Time"); *Volt* ("Woe [I]," "Woe [II]") and *Verse* ("Revenant").

Poems also appeared online in *Bathhouse* ("Jottings"), *Can We Have Our Ball Back* ("Capstone," "Fissure," "Ur-Dissonance"), *GutCult* University of Michigan ("Still Water"); *Jacket* ("Revenant") and *VeRT* ("In the Wake of Fallen Mountains"); in the CD-rom journal *Papertiger* ("It Makes No Difference"); and in the web journal/print annual *Ducky* ("The Director," "Woe [III]").

The Makeshift was released in 2002 in the UK by Stride Books. My gratitude to Rupert Loydell for its publication, and for his unflinching faith in it. Thanks to John Kinsella and Chris Hamilton-Emery for accepting *Accumulus* for publication.

Many thanks to my entire family for their support, and to those who helped these books take shape over the past six years, including but not limited to Brian Henry, Dara Wier, James Tate, Franz Wright, Tomaz Salamun, Forrest Gander, Matthew Zapruder, Peter Richards, Derek Webster, Daniel Nester, Kevin Goodan and Andy Morgan.

The Makeshift

Part I

Having Learned to Sing, I Find it Difficult

The rain is angry today.
   I've done her wrong, she hisses.

No matter.

It's enough to hear her hiss,
   enough to hide in the shattered mirror

of black, black that is this,
   a particularly cold evening,

one in which I'm not allowed to dream –
   no, allowed to regret and to rue . . .

What is there to regret?

Rain – I've become fluent in it.
Rain's an easy difficulty.

Having learned to sing
I find it difficult

to watch her, so much beauty,
trillions of little bulbs of beauty

in fact, come down to me,
   bestow herself to me.

She says she misses her brother –
her lover – oh yes but what about me

Do you miss me

Having learned to sing
I find it difficult

to come back to earth –
I'm a black cloud of notes –

    discordant symphony,

    breath of rain lingering

which much like everything
have no reason or rhyme

but in a little black sack

where they may be viewed
    for all time

Awake, First Light

This moment's been met.

That one,
and that one too:

    The fire.
    The bleak forest.

But I'm not a victim of the fire!

I've never had a moment
in and of
or as
myself

to have been charred
as the skin
of a present soul,

somehow lackluster
in its smoulder.

Episodic

Midnight glow: could it be the gas station? piecemeal serials of holding her / holding her / holding her. Clicktrack. Her lukewhetted smile almost at iron's boiling point. Gallons click away. There are even night-crows in suburbia, honey, see them ply the daggering octane glow? Here – entrails of midnight, – wind fisting my eyes. O was she unaware, my petal backseat, of fragrance dappling down & atwards, –

Man staggered from bath, ate pears, fed hummingbirds / skip a bit // filled tank, danced backalleyway with waitress from Tunisian cargo plane – or Hardee's, more likely. *They all lie about two things,* he grumbled. *Their daddies and their from-whereabouts.*

Apple chest "on" solar-room floor. Apples "within" chest, "apple" within "apples," and all was contained neatly (in mahogany) inside a tiny logjam we might as well call Birthday. For it's heard, said a neighbor who is prone to shaping Bosc pears with jack-knives "into" West Shore Fluttering Hummingbirds, there's a tiny mechanical heart churning beneath these somewheres –

The Root of Everything

I.

The second before the mold,
the green before the green in the grass,
the vanished silence becoming words.

Describe those seconds, those colors,
those transitions, and how slow? how much?
In the scatter of brown and weed,

in the slow strain of yeast,
in the curve of torpid clay,
in each upward reasonlessness

the many mingling shelves of categories.
For instance: Light, and givers of light,
the takers and swallowers of it;

Mechanics of sight and silence,
bright and vanish, gust and breathless,
still lawns, open palms.

II.

Sun, know what I know
from this balcony:
not everything is a painting,

funded and fused,
layered and spackled.
If only everything had such spirit.

Spirit is subdued all around you:
Stars fall silent, bandaged by night,
thinkers go speechless in low candlelight,

and no tree is a bursting tree:
Autumn's a kind of deliberate simmer,
the giving of color mingling with the taking,

like the moment we learned music –
that stirring of several instants

known even by the trees, ever pushing out

toward you.

III.

A girl sings. What is this force?
An orange newt scurries the boulder.
A yellow pair of socks waves in the breeze.

All know toward something,
something the bones say must be,
something the more than bones command.

The newt has a tongue.
The breeze is a fragility full of dust.
What is first apparent is the dust.

The girl has a religion, a secret.
What is first apparent is her voice.
Her secret plumes her voice.

Is there no way to unite these parties?
The girl stands on the beach sidewalk,
the newt is in Patagonia or Mexico,

the socks are filled by another party
who has not much to do with the poem
but everything to do with the breeze.

IV.

I knew a fellow who forgot everything
but woe.

He knew his function: hang quietly,
look disgruntled, be seen

(frilly billows, magenta cheeks like cloudrise)
and not heard, accept his allowance
of spider-spit and sun-silt.

Anyway, they say, he went
somewhere where people
don't even have windows.

They have magma,
and it bleeds everywhere,
keeping the contrasts sharp.

Why opt for enclosure?

Stale, stale, the storefronts
in that fellow's former town.

What else knows the staleness?
No safe guess but every inch of the innermost.

V.

"It would make a cat laugh"
JIPPENSHA IKKU

a. It still would, and his words are 200 years old.
Cats still exist.
Translators still exist.
                    Proof?

Laughter has mutated from a pleasure
to an indictment.
This is my translation.

b. Ikku on the candled evening deck.
Highball on the balcony. Over the railing –
What hangs there before us is too casual.

c. Not to live, not to progress:
To relinquish the nothing,
To blindly grope through the pall.

Reverie

I.

Let's say her eyes are lemoning
like peonies. But she looks

Too quickly: like, for instance, a peak in the Andes:
How its outline fades from memory with each sonic snap

Of each icicle clink
On the aforementioned peak.

II.

On being blessed by silence:

A peak in the Andes, "devastatingly blue,"
A blue not quite *ready*, a migrator –

Some pilgriming censer-bearer of silence.

The swarm of winter in her eyes.

III.

Her eyes were crumbles of lull,
Were they? Once.

During the time of the great snows,
That's when: Then.

Once and Then are intransitive, dual,
Little brown flourishes outside my shutters

That register in the brown paste of my brain.

IV.

        Of a tiny vessel, storm-swept,
irritable,

her stare is the mast.

I'm sorry. My reasoning's
            often blood iron, brain salt,
But bitter-er, by leaps.

V.

Bereft of honey, her stare
simply crept in my pores,
            nestled among guttae.
Simply:
not like honey, more like a wound.

More like a bomb threat –
            a dim-white time
            like a garage bulb
glowing somewhat safely on hammers, crickets,
    tools and lawnmowers.

            Not suburbia, alas, but
a wound,

        she said.

Listen to the blood, not the implications.

Diary

~

I like the word 'furlong' –

~

I will soon begin the habit of reading every page in weekly local trade papers – the kind the postman hangs from the mailbox – voraciously, for I'm aging, and what else to do with age but spend every ounce on such pursuits – scavenging the fine print – whopping sales, free car washes, half-off pizza delivery, press releases, snapshots of elementary school kids visiting nursing homes to sing, hang tinsel garlands —— I've long taken humanity in measured little doses, a blizzard of it now I'll welcome

~

I have a secret hill
  all my own
and there I thought
and came to think
real beauty was
this deep blue
spectre
that turned out
  merely
traffic lights
glazed by fog
that one night
I came to think
about real beauty

~

Real terror – the child asks,
  have I earned it?

I walk among the sick,
          and the child is sure
he's not one of them

for his eyes fix
on the balloon

not on its string

or the little balloon-knot
to which the string is tied

as sky is poisoned

with color, with floating

Friendly things always leaving the earth

The Near-Miss Slides

1. No-one as unreasonable as I,
coolly dipped in frown's aqua regia,
spindled in it, too many bobbins and creels.

2. There is some whirligig word *en aspersa,*
and I've almost caught the elusive thing but it gurgles –
pretty much a protest, elegant and hurt dazzling.

3. Almost finally aced the bugger, I think,
finally shucked the bone of the trouble,
down to the wiry tendrils in un-doubt's helix.

4. Path and re-path have I gone, Lord, cornice
low and hardly sweet; the tree must again be
a tree as well as any truth can grow needles.

5. I can squint away the week, on occasion
my very scaffolding, exiting easily. It is bright here.
The nut from the hazel, breaking out into the bright.

6. "Lament, never written more simply,"
one said on the subway platform – another screamed blight,
while others dribbled as all our fetid eyes, dead eggs adroop.

7. Moths have woven similar trouble. Sockets
are no match for pincers, reliable even in the nave's damp tonsil.
We are warm carriages, warm parcels of surprising shift.

8. Brother, luck be thy parcel; brother,
my hands reprise the tides of youth; they tremble and balloon,
sad flags in a dreaming sky, in a cirrus-milk of youth.

Ghazal

Rejecting the plinth of constriction, involucral dust
spirals away toward freedom: prodigal dust.

Rotor equals praetor, *course* equals *lost*;
conceal the tract of truth, o pellicle dust.

In Wichita, a carnival showman connives,
peddling his stockpile of "Miracle Dust."

She smells of hyacinth. She gloats adrift
the seiche of forgotten god and oracle – dust.

Your neighbor's love-seat hoards like a tenement
snippets of memory, mites and follicle (dust).

Ever so acute in this box we call sunset
an angle of copper, a cacodyl dust.

Bottles of vintage: diluted Thames,
Yangtze. In the carburetor: pebbles, Halical dust.

So say we all this day, Ethan: the scion
will feather and burn as caracul dust.

Note to Myself: On Self-Importance

Moved to write about cockatoos,

forgetting to finish one tract about ribbons
and buttons,
       the other about mixing cocktails
using cherry purée and celery stalks,

eschewing the results of a nationwide poll on soap abuse,

lingering in the "meadows of one's youth" done up in pen
and ink on a greeting card,
                      you laugh

– and laugh heartily.

There is no one around to hear you laugh!
                             Why do it, then?

Paintings in a gallery don't run around like children,
yearning to be caught, yelling "Look at me!"

Sculptures in a rock garden don't avoid shadows,
because they know: Darkness is good for the complexion.

And tea bags are tiny not without reason:
They like to hide out, behind crockery and dried flowers.

Best to pay attention to the polished granite faces
and portraits of soldiers, heroes and saints;

to listen duly to the moan of the modest tea bag
you squelched with thumb and spoon.

You will be forgotten someday, a cockatoo.

Bolus

The trick is in keeping that one bolus is not "better"
or more elastic, or chewier, than another. *On n'est pas comme
l'autre.*
Still, there's eeriness in any ordinary bolus, this you know:

That bolus X stews in a vial with cabbage and carrots,
tasting of yesteryear and burnt-sugar, the rinds of castaway
grapes,
and narrates a legacy greater than any hand or pen or cave wall;

That bolus Z is no more mealy than your retinal discord,
the caldera in your stomach, the lymphatic gnosis your eyes
corral
in the vernal seascape – lone boats, toss'd umbrellae, ad inf.

~

Still, there's eeriness in the bolus, any of them, the spit out
and the swished, the wiped and the dribbled. The bolus of
Woman
is often an hourglass bolus. It is usually petaled, and rosé.

The bolus of Man is trinitial, an only-begotten bolus, the Keeper
of Humanity bolus: dark and sulfured: contoured as a candlepin,
and almost as lithe and fraiche when toupéed and powdered.

There arise so many problems with gradients and pressure in the
chaw
that scientists huddle in backrooms discerning the bolus
parabola.
The funny-men imitate bolus pie-fights for late night popcorn
time.

~

There is something liberating in discussing the bolus: serious,
    less,
than usual: composed, more: writing about the lumps have we
    known:
The lumps of our lives, our roadways, our constancies and
    driftings,

our Arizonas and Mount Pleasants, our soul-mates and affairs,
our security-camera operators and the flagons in the alpinia,
our tepid, yellow teeth and fat ties in company presentation
    rooms.

Bolus, when I think *disaster* and *lovelorn*, *woebegone* or *academia*,
my head is washed in gentle frost. I know we are all-American
    originals,
longing for gentle, weightless spaces in the margins or middles,
    that's all.

More Like Montpelier

n^{th} triggered sunset, tripwire 7 PM,
capriccio flourish of darkness
I always wrote to you about, yawning.

Fractures of grackle
& phone wire angle,
furnishing the skyward scenery well-
enough for God, that flat pleasure
steaming through stucco'd weepwinds.

Here, aesthetics well-
avoid most of Plato's
ideals: kitsch plastic vines,
bistros' red checkers, lazy-susans
offering with dynamic robotix
an assortment of oil and ointment.

Never like this in my mind.

Spelling bee kids' minds. Or more
accurately, geography kids' minds,

those who knew it was a state capital
and laughed up milk on fiberglass trays.

Have you heard? I'd ask. Factorial quotas
spawned new four-pocketed models. They're sharp.

One pocket for pea combos, one for salads
and for the others, porkish saltdrizzle
– but anyway,

it's hard to hear myself hear you tell me to ask
whether it's lake-effect romance or sanguine & perfumed,
the kind before pornographers made us look at trees differently.

Here, I don't notice too much.
Mostly I talk to snow, asking for directions.

I wear lamps in snow storms, looking for sleep.
Parks are empty. Bricks are washed. Birds, none.

What I know of your sleep: weeds, sprig-wheeze.
You told me: resigned in the window, arms crossed,
cigarette. I saw this from the lawn and wondered,

wondering *what is it I cannot afford here.*

Apostasy

Chestnut sky
  and lunch with X,
speaking over the crush of Main Street:

humming engines, humming strutters
  skimming the brick,
flashing tattoos, flagging cabs.

Another humdrum canticle.

Mid-noon flue, burst,
  sun splayed on City Hall.

Then from clouds drizzled by God
like a soupy tempera
            – misty, cumular billows,
                      onionskin up there, almost

– nothing ever as luminous as that YELLOWNESS,
  that stark headache yellow:

beamed-down revelation of a fraudulent life,
  yes, a sad but not
entirely unexpected moment . . .

I'd planned for that moment – finally it'd come –

I'd cut my canvases in half,
  fearing the many years of downpour . . .

What a scene –

our modern Noahs scurrying
into camper-trucks
    made of glass.

Then the bee plague:

stinging us for our own good,
    for being so self-occupied while
God huddled up there, lonely.

How dare we, I told X

but he was gone, had
    walked off
had been enveloped –

One day will he find healing
    in the uncontrollable
beauty of not this world

Sonata

How swept with calamity, outer cosmata,
we equate it with "we" and feel coffinite,
we sense *sense* and sense it is id over up,
down over frailty
and likeness versus backlash.

Rou-tou-tou, chiming tirade,
pitches in flux, inflection,
the hand-held sophists' graphite practices,
mirrors and lecterns,
the cage-keys to a poached fetiduum,
their breath.

Beyond the vastness of what used to be the galehead

Beyond the golden robe that granite spake like oft wild
drownings

(Where were the drownings?)   And now
there are two drownings,
spatial in character,
for he said
they were
six miles apart
over the lustre bridge,
pins keeping time for fog.

Lingerings Near Southern April

Fog, a cupping nutshell, dirging the land,
may or may not gain weight ahover, pondering –

Sun-jaws spidering down, septicians in wet repentance,
must know the soul of the grasses, the wish for the kind of soul

in clovers, stretching brainless for surrection, safe from fire;
    Knowing the fire,

saint of glow in a strange ocean full of vagrant saints,
anointed petals in a still chamber, washed with so much
    nothing,

    who would blame them,
dangling caesura one jump's millionth away.

   ~

Too much blindness in the world – you can catch it at Village
    Swamp
if you're not wearing waders.

Veins feed the thing, fourteen square miles,
dun-sullied pinnipeds, froth basking in solar triangles,

those stutter-steps light takes, hesitating,
clipping that bough and that one there,

again and again, coal-fed, forever plying.
Veins, unseen but undoubted, taken on faith –

a pearl jewel moves, wrote Li Yu,
one senses strange perfumes

– undercut, back hand the froth-rot,
indeed, a lurking perfume.

≈

So it is with the obituaries. I sat all day and wrote their lives up,
this Last Biographer. "*John X is liquid now,*" else he floats

in pleasant drapery, one of stark, cardinal red. That I wrote
A and not B, C and not D, does it displease? In this "glomerulus,"

this "humanity," are there not in-roads for fabrication,
convex aberrations, dents in a bee-line glance?

≈

Erase it all, the muddy season beckons.
　　Erase, erase.

Here is movement in the cinders, the old blasted oak. Light-
ning shook its splinter to soot, its bark to cloud; trance,

a stale sanctuary, somewhere grotto-dark. Here is noting
the simplicity of words: few syllables: their near-pantomime act

is an oxen pack, ruffled by April, its molassia, its decline
in the humble shadows on Lake (or *Pool*) _____.

Noma that is the east, east in morning's sill,
doctor that is happenstance – the luck of curtain-corners left
　　apry

　　– here is transfusion,
the loudest of prescriptions.

Laughter is X, Laughter is Y

I.

I had to get there quick to see it:
Harry's pursuit for the perfect umbrella,

the graying myriads plying the naiads
at Flought Beach for dimes and ice nuggets

(which spell the flume of hot dough and frankfurter
almost enough to keep the bikiniads pleasant),

thongs re-routing the glances of *a.* Hopper
                                 b. Rockwell
                                 c. Winslow

  [*it is said that, depending on their infirmity,*
  many of them choose to "go by" their last names]

; those becapped men we've known to frequent the strip,
who claim there's nothing to top the sensation
                                   of denture cream *down there.*

II.

Well, I told some old friend the story,
mailed it to him, I think; I even affixed an Expressionist
poster-replica –
I do not think it was Lautrec –
of an absinthe bottle – it was not Degas, either –
half-drunk
; the cigars stood out, though
; every dapper gent gripped one professionally,
somewhat confidently, even the casual observer might add.

III.

There are simply the old men with gray back hair walking the
plankstrips at Flought Beach, men who "fought wars, strained
their backs lifting hay bales, and wielded the mute tools of a gener-
ation," who ever reflect on that shaky spell:

when Maman's whisper splayed the air, the Gospel in the pantry
louder than hearts recently aneurysed; when grass tracked in by
Father would ever live as a chalk on the wind.

IV.

(His response, an extraneous letter I called _A Maiming_)

I hung the Expressionist absinthe bottle next to the typewriter.
I was told Lautrec by the passive voice of the Apartment C2 bank-teller
. . . or is she the surgeon?
Well, anyway, I was glad to know we still have the same taste in art,
but the question remains: will we ever break bread again,
sup on the primrose <vin> again?

V.

There is a grove in Oregon that supplies walking canes
     for 90.3% of Americans.
There is a grove further north, in Alberta, that supplies
     canes for 79% of Canadians.
The grove is the loudest grove you've ever seen.

On Flought Beach, I was struck by the dim eyes of old men,
     holding firm on mine,
their stares like cats underfoot, like night studying
     decomposition –
because it's born bandaged and scratches at all of us,
     underneath.

Everyone's given up on that now, all umbrellae are folded
for the eve. Look the tide is out – even God has given up.

The Makeshift

Tonight, God, I ask the deafened rush of the leeshore.
The moon is tethered from its smoky wince
and means to whisper sullen lyrics to earth's nape:

Allow it to breathe this loveletter, celestial dobbin
smote with the effort of coals, spirate and spitting,
this final gift that would sear the auric tinge off night.

Look through the window: I am a keen scientist.
Texturalis lemon, vague chapterhouse in the eyes
that burns each moment I paint, casting out its lodgers.

Never, not with tidal insistence, or *bons mots*
curled and kempt (staid in tulle) from Reason,
will the moon sidle toward *wish*: stoic dobbin,

hauling without benefit of purge's siege,
if it can indeed be purged of anything at all:
the moon is very light without needing to stand ashore.

It's not diuretic, not addictive, not bereft of penalty,
nor does its flapping tarpaulin indicate sturdy epoch,
the kind *here*: "The ocean berates the cliffs."

Flourish, brief concertina of moonbreak.
Never-intended music.

All told, it's fissured and mantic, our season's dyssemia.
Pray for pockets where aphids nest in sleep's golden jaw,

plying daybreak for a nether's hand of dust, warmth,
remittance of anything resembling nocturne or cloud,

skying the absence of accume where strati strike
as scowls, above and so far and hatingly above.

The Mandarin

INTERPRETER

When glancing in sleep, any riddle's boxed
out: night's dry calamine is a foreboding heat.

Listening has breathed into the riddle more than usual.

Naked, how your unsolve whittles at my reserve;
the blemish left behind is an empty parlor, laughter.

When glancing you in sleep, any taph
is fair game: *bio, ceno, oro, epi.*

If you can feel a laughing, are you wrong?
Steam, freightage.

Without bulk, dreams control no aspect
of their trace; without the kill,

linger is as much a lie as a ribbon, dainty waif.

NOT THIS, MIRROR

I am not the setting-foot onto railway's expanse,
not the Father's dun dead, splinter of fortune

or one of these timely, silvery chimes bloom't
rounder, rounder even than surf billows.

I am a musteline prowling the lacunae
of an earthquake.

My kind, my kind, who is now not my kind?

I am made in the likeness of dust,

custard, downed in a pinch,

an ear-mark in a lusty chapter.

≈

1. The sum of 2. pallid skin and fright reaches for
        3. disinterment
and 4. other flights.

I have 5. been advised to lose 6. my cadence here,
        this being a holiday 7. week and all.
Floorboards squirm,

the sink's a victim 8. of rat-rummage, same for
9. the cupboard.
        10. "Incubus is never so cold as lechery,"

11. the clatter says. "Her heart won't know enough
      12. to sprout haunt and distrust"

13. – and then, is done with it.

In blameless black,
      guilt backs into prongs and flame.

My grainy pleasure floats, a fugue,
      forever *16.* a fugue – soft, broken dayscape.

The surf dies.

      ∼

I'm compelled to twist day's petals.

I've wrung them sufficiently, got it all
down to this hopeful southern hour,

scriptmute with wrists and branches.

I bet exploration is not in the meeting
but in the erasing:

the skull-sheen nods.

Two Hypotheses

whether conium is poisonous
depends on the flighty *nasale*

trepidated as a schematrix
who has foregone the medial

and reckoned even bigger pursuits:
counting wicker in corner stores,

counting whiskers at yellow noon,
counting holes in the seraphic looks

which pine depthly from arc'd lady-stares

∾

(did i ever describe to you the left
in the diffidence between your here

and my there and all belatedness)

when you squirmed enjoyment made its own
niche like felled waterlog'd newsprint likened

without prejudice to many smiles

did i forget to bridge the mention restless
for no stir's as gelid as sky disarmed of its air

or such rampancies as marblish stratus

no offense in your left, it's got to go somewhere
out the wayback, on a wayfront, wayside's

not the place for it's too much in view

stones as eyes, here's the uneasy in describe
for i rappel down its slatesides in slow burn

eaten by the consume in your left, your gone

Apogee Brevita

I was nearly plied from my black sack
(man-hole from "the time being")

but the world's bit is zinc and harsh –
stammer, now, choke out, now –

and keeps me plaintive: like black
drawing its reminder over us,

my body walked off, deserted
the finest city of all, bitter light.

Part II

A Vision, Winter

Through the syrup of night, trees – over there.

Beauty approaches with knocked-out teeth.

Hard to persuade someone who refuses to admit
to the jeweled tang
  of their piss –

but I'll try. She's *looking for me.*

She's not looking for anyone else. I know this.

Swing, fat ballerina,
                    you've gained weight.

I'll see you through the lean times –
  diets, forced vomiting, the like.

On my back I wear a child's piano –

Tinkled notes of midnight, crisply frozen grass

Flight Pattern

A bombed suite

Scarless rise into morning
or . . . morningless scar

Still photographs
    feather the jaw of this room

I saw you buried in sun's empty

In bedazzled crows
    with square rules
for silence

To a Child Not Yet Afraid of the Dark

Night balances on your head,
   waiting for the end.

Every time the sun goes down
   it's a not-real end

for it's there yet again
   when your blood's boyish,

when your piss's welled up,
   when the bird furnace –

daybreak pouncing crows
screaming sparks –

sparks are not-real fire –
   just as dark is not-real end.

Just as skin's a not-real surface –
   just one that's artfully executed –

Artfully executed, Thank God,
   or you'd *know* the dark, child,

you'd really know it, the legions
   (See: Expired bulbs, walking millions of)

Like the Song Goes. "There's a Man With

a gun over there." Now, we must ask
whether that's a *soi-disant* worldview,
said Q, who lunched with me frequently.

We'd eat as if we worked in cardboard,
our dusty factory around the café's corner,
the shift commander and union steward

shouting from the top steps, Come back,
come back. Croissants – put them down, you.
The cardboard is laden with water, and limp.

Q's was an insight not of the ex-professor
who wrote a pamphlet on "JOHN-PAUL SARTER"
but of a man with collard salad, eating unsatisfied.

Study of Three Men With Faces Painted
by Francis Bacon

Open letter to my landlords three: your surnames, as I read them
all nice & hyphenated on your business cards, remind me of a law
firm that advertised not in Idaho. Fix my sink.

Lovely Lily smoked on the patio, and you called:
Against all fire zoning laws she smokes, you all said.
I could feel the gelid craws of your teeth.
I believed your anger was a burned field of brick,
the weight of winter driving its fence-rungs down.

On my cousin's birthday, the first day he straddled a pony, the first
day he downed a highball, you all came with shovels. Clean up
after your pony, and the cat, you all said.

In the little bulb of mercury, which I deftly velcro'd
to the aluminum window-casing on the house's east side,
I first noticed your briefcases curved as Lily's previous breasts;
and then noticed, after a nibble of potato salad, the wash upon
your faces three, white as Paris, eyes dazed as pigeons

or infants seeking to look inside or upward for once, fancying
themselves as rodents or shingles. Fancying myself a betting man
I know the game is up, and not just because your hands are bliz-
zards of crows & can't deal.

Rural Notebook

Wait – smell, now – spice of crabapple, straw.

Fucked once in this orchard, I think.

My chest, pewter & matchsticks;
hers, dull tocsin of night-sparrow.

It's true, a fuck in an *orchard*? – but the hands had left.

Rotten fruit culled, they retired for the night while I stealthed into
    her.

And no father would foresee it: fucking in an orchard's deflated air,
    gasp on sky, lily on skywater.

   ~

To name after a deceased wife: use prepositional phrase,
allude to birds or pink lozenges and tea savored on noondecks
near an Adirondack camp or isle of shoals.

"But what of the vanilla coffee and orange extract,"
one might ask. "*Nothing* resembled those, and everyday
in her breath and soft manner?"

Hawks in the air, hawks on the ground, circling.
Bones of an interlude, particularly blanched.

Textures of Domesticity

I.

With drang and clack,
aim for the dry cochlea,
some deadened chrome home-iron,
its burn-drooled pressingboard
cornered in a closet.

II.

Suffused
with lilaciate stench,
tempered
with upturned edge
and pleut-swells
from November snow,
it plies the therms
of passing trucks
into diesel-sodden ditches,
cemeteries of bruised protest.

III.

Adenine, the ague of walls.
Pale and partisan,
the drawn-out shudders
of the kitchen littoralis
are mornings of dark conch,
forgotten tones of pear
in a sprawling lawn,
the mitigated glance of glaive and knife.

Rooms, Steadily Darkening

For long – your touch, its stanched matté (a collar of weeds).
Now it's come to this: talk of balconies, anchors, pinions,
their eddies assaulting the placid ethos of the kitchen.

Balconies betray darkness, it must be; and anchors always
imply the scuttled and stalled, and pinions – well, why *not*
        pinions?

The side-room is draped blue, all over and warm. Not indigo
but blue, not passion but warmth, and even then a remittance.

Cold transaction, kitchen's bathure into that warm side-room.
Cheap, in ways. Tile, corkboard.

Lucky to have been there while light quibbled hoarsely with
        bedboard.
I know the fugitive now.

The color of egg, I know you wait for just one strand to stand
in disagreement.

Entries Fitted for Freezing Rain

I.

My wife told me, for my health, I must subsist on spirolina
    mosses.

                  I've never heard of them.

                  Are they eaten by what Karavis
                  called 'the minute thrushlings
                  that misplace / the sun'?
                            Perhaps
                  I misplaced the line break.
                            Perhaps
                  I misunderstood the poet's
                  terror,
                        caught in a snow of thrush
                  and a lace of sun.

II.

My son told me I am a thin poet.

                I was overheard, by his friends,
                muttering in a classroom.

                        My speech
was mud.
                        The thin light
was vine.

                It curved blindly, but his friends,
                they saw the light knew where to go,
                        knew where to fill me.

III.

My object told me I have the stare of an unknown.

My favourite object,
quiet as bread.

Daring me to finish
my sentence.
My scene.

Sad

The party we've all been to

Someone eating cheese
   right off the knife

Someone comparing himself
   to the ornament forgotten
on the tree

Discarded at the curb

When but for a bit of effort
   and a keen eye

He could have been saved

For next time, the next
go round

And you wish you could say

There is no next go round
because fire has torched
the possibilities

Because night –

Went and did it didn't you

Made the people sad – made them

    turn away and here you are

One knife on the counter

No one in the room

Box

I've removed my smile
and hung it on another

who is quite content
to serve my soul

as its capsule –

Content, like rain
  drenching the girls –

They can't fool us with their dance –

Who is there to elude the rain

Canned Cloudscape

Deadwood grove – she dangles her first kiss in a creek.

Her supple hair, lubed to a wisp, like tin in landing-lights.

Virgo to Pisces: "Miles apart
                              . . . miles apart."

There are preludes – and there are *preludes* –

smell of steak in winter   *what of it?*   streaks on a window,

birds on furlough: the unfold designed. Sculpture of error.

Some things shall never be reconciled. Believe it.

I have borne clay-tinged water – have hated my yoke.

I have been swallowed by clay-tinged water –
                                    strangled . . .

She's a fraction   *an assemblage*   her kiss is glue,

tinsel a-melt   *birds aloft by wire*   they can't cross

paths   *miles apart but the start of a new field*

Terrarium, a Quincunx

Instruments. – Alternately, these crack and measure the smile, willing you / nilling you. There are lessons: how miniature shovels, the ones used for digging repens from the side of a highway, can be turned toward your chest by a raving grandmother. Following seizures she'd speak of stagecoach wheels, as well, instruments for raccoons or turncoats who embezzled gold from some foothills cabin to fear. She was lucid in the screen-porch, the hat of a tiny girl fallen in a pond. Lucid's as good as a smile, a sound diagnosis.

Their hats on a pond o pray they fall not in.

Passersby watched from a coach these transgressions: walking on water, cursing the wind.

A chorus of tiny girls in polkadot clamdiggers –

terrible sighs the noises of flush, a coachful of sprightly vague weight

or:

i think we're afraid o yes we're afraid of night it hangs from our necks

or:

an octave dispatched by weather will settle on this bank

Somewhere there is a calm garden, and a shovel to turn under the many thin bones of these dreams.

Another version:

Dear children led through a garden's erupting lilies. Learned the word 'splaying' – as in cirrus, which did so in the form of smiles.

Path of cloud hovers, not cloud itself,

– a wake.

All the bus-ride children in their green seats bore witness to *version* for the first time.

There was lily, a poison, abandoned letter. There was the bone hearth of earth. There were sleeves of thorns for all to wear, for those outside to leer upon.

"None of us were born there," Suze said of _____. She could have been talking about the fishbowl. It teetered on the sink as Herve filled it with fertilizer – dried rabbit shit, which can be had for a song at any local rabbitry. The finest is that of the New Zealand rabbit (the white kind), which incidentally suffers hock-scurvy very easily. Care must be taken to wash its feet daily. The Chinchilla's shit retains more oxygen, for they have 2–3 extra centimetres of small intestine. Lops don't shit much – and placed the salamander inside the small ceramic castle. It looked like the abandoned textile mill being demolished in favor of a pharmacy. Pharmacies are springing up everywhere. "None of us were born into this shit," said Suze, peering out the screen-porch at heavy traffic. The salamander curled in the sun of its little fishbowl, shit-ions commuting the vacancies of hot evening air.

One Field

I drove a lawnmower atop a wasp-nest,
shearing it.

I ran from the garden (trellis)
to barn (beams, bales).

The run was a ball coursing a plane
of glass.

The glass wanted hopelessly to contain
the run of the ball.

The glass was magnolial in tincture
and radial in juncture.

The barn was a lightning rod visible
only through glass.

Visibility was a matter of seismism
for the ball was rattling matter –

the chase was an agent of rattle, you see
– and my bones I could hear through the wasps.

The Use of Reinhardt
(Stations of the Cross)

Morning revealed bunting –

draped and tacked
on branches, mailboxes,
swaying
     there . . .

Know the old wounds
will seep in again.

Melancholia

My hero rode a horse. My adoration for him
went beyond his horse or horselessness, even.

It's a story: coral. So much niche-whirling,
so many miles of blue summertimes.

Hooded and veiled, he'd been a darkness-receptor
in a placid wheatfield. Then he went *swim, swim.*

Swimming into places no one had been before.
Swimming like prayer. Quietly – like reeds, or noon.

I'm inspected by darkness. It tells me I'm 'good.'
But this is a knoll which the moon will avoid,

where each day is a horse that's bereft of its haul,
where one wouldn't find my hero caught dead.

ORIEL

Put your best forward first –
the way this whirligig "is"
on the edge of an oriel.

There's a point, see?
The way we kissed trees
knew which wind stir'd.

Light is God's first mistake.
The way was lighted for us
these many humans atumble.

But on the edge of an oriel
we made our kisses airy the way
trees tumble in mistaken fog.

MÖBIUS IN WIND

The field as if a trial.

The brought as forgotten, omen of children.
Dancing children, as if dance were borne of not here.
Children dance in the wind here.

No children dance in the fetters of wind.

The wind was in another city,
coursed through another's shutters,
did not course through my city.

My city is a dust flotilla.

Dust dances not in dust but as dust,
as children dance in children and not as children,
unaware of their childness as the wind of its guilt

as it courses the field, any field.

Final Days of the Affair

These are bones.

My bones are a blue village from my dreams;
I walked there with my love in a cool frost,

Saw cool-fringed trees on the outskirts.
Tired of the cold she settled in the trees.

I am the sound of a man leaving town.
I am the sound of ash choking a dream.

Journeyman, a Reverie
Spanish lowlands, _____

Under the stars, I crossed a river,
crossed the sound of the river being crossed –

my feet in traverse,

my ears primed for clack
and the swish of my feet.

I walked over the bridge in Ecija.

"What bridge in Ecija?"

It is there, it is there. Fear not; that is for children.

At this hour, we feel the happiness of a child
who does not yet understand darkness.

∾

I walked over the bridge in a corner of town known for its shadows. Old women place their sacks down on the stone streets and rest on patches of grass. Sometimes birds shriek from old cypress trees lining the cramped boulevard, which is rife with vendors and carts. The color of fruit is something I never knew until Ecija. The color of Utrera: no color. After boarding there for several weeks, the color of my hair darkened, and a dull woman said my face had flattened. The mirror spoke, but I was inextricably captured by dumbness. Utrera's grays and whites – floating in the sky, imbued in the stone of churches and shops, flickering in the flags and linens of vendors, in the eyes of geese – afford the strangest drowsiness.

~

The bridge must have beckoned me. It was made of gold granite, and spanned the Genir. In the twilight, one could read a sign cemented into the chinked rock:

Tenemos corazones resistentes y las almas

My eyes wandered more than usual. It was liquid night – the hour dark as slate, little men sitting along the riverbanks blowing softly into flutes. The stars and the notes swirled together, dancing in unison, wafting ashes. The cobbled path leading toward the bridge wound past a public garden, the fountain deserted but for several young people, quieter than my dreams. Cypress trees stretched high into the chill. I heard the dull woman say my face had melted into the cold air. Dull woman, I want to ask you if you have taken a lover and, if so, if the thought of his spilling hair drowns you.

~

My son ran home happily, bursting into the kitchen. He said he'd fallen in love with a girl. He told of how she stood in a crowd at a parade, how he noticed her cheering, and the glint of a yellow balloon tethered to her wrist.

～

Ecija is hot with noon, which rises in waves over the hilltops and spills on vendors' carts, making their horses anxious. A small bridge, made of masonry block quarried from northern hills before the war began, reaches over the Genir. One gets a sense that the earth has slowed to a lull in Ecija. God draws a blanket of flies, sweat over the city. Old men play dice in the street, in the dust. Patrons seek refuge beneath merchants' canopies. I look toward the river where my son once played with friends, where he fell from a boulder and lacerated his chest. He cried, poor boy, for many hours, refusing to sleep. I sheltered him in my bed that evening. Now I look toward the bridge, blurred in the blast of heat, and pray for winter, for ice to still this river, this sweat.

≈

There is no sense mourning your son today, one of the old men told me. *Your black clothing will char you*. The bridge is the coolest place in Ecija. Looking into the Genir, my hands quivering and my eyes wavering between a passing flock of ducks and a stick floating down-stream, a sense of dusk overcomes me. What! in this heat? I'm not an imbecile to sense a darkness within my bones, to feel it stir. I am watching the Genir flow downstream in the heat of mid-summer, bathing in the hearth of San Gil bridge, summer sinking, an extinguished rose.

≈

My son is gone, in another room. The bridge is unlike any room: all that closes in, comes closer, is the stream below, beginning in the mountains, passing beneath your feet on its way to somewhere slower.

Wanderer

Shadows dangle on the pallid alder. Swing
themselves from facade to facade.

Your laugh moved like that –
$\qquad\qquad\qquad\qquad$ I boxed it . . .

I can't explain the cold

– perhaps, a little box adrift
on a rough gray sea

Just Before Diversion

Look how the rain defines its own path,

not like the way it would be in my palm –

the rain in my palm would circle, as if refusing

to let the fence of a gaze restrict it, as if motion

across the tracks: I've seen a luncheonette lady,

stealing but a click to look for the little rain-storm

she might conjure someday, over some little knoll

with a cellular tower, knowing that conjuring

a slight breeze, one neither hither or thither, resolved

to blow and only blow, is much like the way nothing much

has reason or rhyme – flutter of tickertape, tangled bristles

on a centipede's spine, the name and lack-of-name

of hard weeds in a former garden.

Dead July

Thunder Over Louisville

Did you come last night

       but at least the lighthouse light
swung around the sky a bit, a bit
of a consolation on my lonely grass

                       so even if you didn't

     ~

There can be no lighthouse here, house,
       girl, branch, . . .   I'm in Louisville, the city the
legend in which I've never set foot.

Ha! But it's fine, really, *really!*   I have a wife
       I don't even know
so Louisville is like a second-home, my homeland.

     ~

Distress, distress:

Distress!

Stand alone in distress,

                    it's white as   but not as white   it's
shrinking across my head

      ~

Head left o dark white distress call shrinking across

                 its
distress a not-so-evident placard in this, God's True Night

Self-Portrait with Quiet Cirrus, Dusk

Are you sure, God?

But I don't remember how to sleep.

It may not be the wisest decision.

Of course I'd never – I mean, I never meant.

You'd have to ask her.

He's gone now.

The sound away from him fell, like chaff.

Even the dream will not bring him back.

I will let myself not sting by his eyes.

Sounds like he's somewhere.

Poem I've Written, It –

like a boulder's
split energies there-

in the image of a sea-going
girl dangling but from not
rigging, from a fire – perhaps
it can move forward with what,
surprises?

When I Don't think of this World

I.

If I were to leave like a cloud
I would become a cliché – I would
become ashamed of my rosy cheeks
and my covering the stars with mist
when, at that one hour, the plants breathe
and down, down go all the aspirations –

II.

To see planets, to catch june-bugs.
Saw no sign of ocean. Saw my face
as a brick. Everything's safe when
you're heavy.

III.

May I take this opportunity, reader,
to tell myself: Don't take your life
so seriously? Be more like the red
spontaneous devil-bug of Australasia.
One morning you shall not wake up
so do it quietly; don't disturb those
peeper-ghosts outside the window,
waiting for your departure, to scoop
the dust from your bed and cast it –

IV.

Breasts by moonlight! Not many other
men have seen my wife's breasts. None
have seen them in this kind of light . . .
They're kind of a joke, really, lonely
little mileposts. And I: hitchhiker.

Having No One Else to Turn To,
I Consult the Night Hour

Think you'll find I'm as makeshift as it gets.

Think of the Lone Man, that sad concept,
thumbing in the dark, dull moon above
all, highway and regrets.

I set off with a withered face.

All the while the moon is chiming softly:
"Look at you, putting out in the dark like a dory!
The night is so beautiful when it quivers for you."

Gone Music

You got me thinking: how it is to remember how we all used to worship and adore the single stray hair left by our lover on a pillow, a collar, an old backpack she rested against on a warm August mountain

How we'd thank God for the gift – being able to smell her after she'd left, being able to drown in her warm touch – being able to tuck the memento into our favorite novel or hidden shoebox

and that by remembering, an implicit burial has taken place somewhere along the line, the exact point perhaps unknown, perhaps guessed after hours of solitary memoriam – "Christ, I don't *feel that way* anymore,

what the fuck *happened to me?*" Not a good feeling, veering toward melodrama . . .

Yes, you said, but even worse to not let it fuck with you – *do not take dying so personally*, the big death and all the little ones on the way

Like an Empty
after Chuang Tzu

Petals learn to live with that black center
of the flower, which has gone nameless

The condition of identifying with a rock
plashed with a river all day, all aeon long

has gone nameless as well

I find myself not as interesting
as these – yet I was granted a name –

Imagine what the petals or river would
think of this lack of human priority

(a condition, incidentally, also nameless)

Wistful

Once I was a left
      and she couldn't explain me to her friends . . .

Then I thought stone was more noble

  so decide, recede

     I did

and from beneath my cool surface called,
     "Is this the way to best serve you . . . "

From Angles

GOD

                                    From here, He is insufficient.

                        Now here, dimly lit.

            Over
              here, poorly drained.

                            And here, rough-
                        hewn.

                To this side, hidden by heliopsis.

    Nope, not there – the ringhals will suffocate Him
and He looks unshaven here in this light.

                                    It's sunset
and some painters are not painting.

They douse stupidly on the lawn in unison.

CURASSOW

Not content with *bird* or *pheasant*,
a Dutch nomenclaturist angled
and her jackpot: *curassow*.

Cracidae.

Eiland vogel.

Fazant met staart.

Tongues, though fancy, can't conjure a bird. To wit:
Crax alector.

Crax alector.

MEADOW

Southeast Corner
   spoketrack, journal and huckaback rucksack.

Southwest Corner
   – the snow affix'd to grass wantonly, choosing its spots,
   dusting here and blasting there.
   – potent July of grass.
   – tomato rows, willowtrunk, lovemaking patch, condos.

Northwest Corner
   Jesu, quem velatum nunc aspicio,
   Oro fiat illud quod tam sitio.

Northeast Corner
   here's where it will end up, if it be so meted.

Hearing Music Through Dark Trees

I imagine this is a movement the owl loves!

He's off delighting in the fluttery notes,
the way they nuance from silence to moonlight,

fluttering upward like beetles in sunlight,
which left us some hours ago.

~

Sunlight's a miniature trawler that plows through the nothing
God handed us, willed us,

which He meant for us to fill with hazy notions and words

and sometimes, as by a camp fire with friends and guitar,
    laughter

and sometimes, as in a broken room,
    the scrape of screaming

and all the time, little blissful owls, or other animals and birds
    I can't imagine at this moment.

~

I can't imagine the other animals, birds, . . . – my apologies.

The owl has had its way with me;
    it has drawn over me a musick irrevocable,

    humming of an hour of moonlight,
humming of an hour of moonlight.

Revenant

if the son is dead,
if the music, dredged –

if the granite is cool,
not charged with heat –

if I speak forthright,
but my mind's on Spain

(really, aren't we all off some-
where like Spain, sea of dust) –

if words reject covenance
with their meanings –

if trees reject their leaning,
leaves forego their revenance –

if rains flush the rust
to thus bear my face – come

back, skin, hide no longer – *rain,
you loner, backdrop, backlight,*

if you'd only quit your retreat –
then the world be awrap in tulle,

stippled colour of the failed,

colour of bells drowned

Problem, Explained, Answered

This mother blinks, then
that, if

you will and perhaps you have heard of that
which is called synchronic

which is that which is best.

The poets rely on words as the urchin, the scuttled hull.

～

There is no room
for you here
is some semblance of room for you.

I'd will an entire estate because I like your eyes
in which I'm a milky semblance of some man off
in somnabulus.

Affix an asterisk for you
don't get it. Don't you sleep, too?

～

There is never breezes in your poems,
are never breezes. No lush total
fissure for you're some man of mind.

Men of mind wander fro yet
never to stop.

There're hives around them but their eyes
betray the incessant wandering.

~

The Director

I think the sun's getting somewhere
beyond this challenging brownstone

and, yeah, I see the sun's cushioned
in a particular way between buildings
when I swing my head just so –

                        it leans like a rebel,

for it hates its portrayal in the flick
by the young and haughty director –

he made it a hero.
                He made who a *what?*

No one wants to be a hero, director!

        Director?

(fiddling with the reel, chiaroscuro,
one reel tumbles, now two – ...

sugary crumbling and

       all our notions sugary

crumbling

       through his daring vision)

Anteros

Poems you wrote about your hair –
I fuck myself when I read them.

I want to never meet you.
Leave you in this perfect state,

free of stain and – moss, smoke.
See, I like the pitter of halyards

on a windy night, Canadian night,
and I never want to see the masts

in your eyes, diamond-float of stars
dusting your brunette curls.

Lead me to my peculiar silence.
Leave me in the low, dark littoralis.

High Horizon

I don't ever want to go back down that Somerset Road, no
with its high, high smokestack my idea of The Countryside

ruinous as a mortar to gouda. Pointing out the blue smell
I ignored you sadly enough and happened upon the poem

in the smokestack. – And anywhere there is an "access road"
there is a disgust. Oblique roads need not calléd attention

so I assume the worst – pits, rusted barrels, carcasses – act
of hiding any and all of the above off some dead end –

and motoring along the Somerset Road to a kiddie carnival
past cornfields poked by driveways to torn-out farmsteads

long vaporized up, bought out, caved in, torn down, whatever
preposition applied, I proposed to you the beauty of varied

leaves. The ones tumbling in a southerly lake dusk. You
must know that off behind this all there was a lake, right?,

a lake,

a lake.

Capstone

"We're all frauds"

ANON.

One of those back roads, the day you wanted to go to the diner, the best diner you'd eaten at, on one of those winter days when sun goes for the eyes (knock-out punch), glaring, gritting its teeth, readying, daring us to drive right into it – we did – yet welcoming enough with its veil of slurred white,

was, I think – I think it had to have been around one of the bends, where they built that controversial bike path (remember the town meeting, Special Session? so many turned up in home-made knit-wear) – the exact location of my Leap Into Manhood, which is to say my first moment of cynical actualization –

Hey maybe I'll teach with a Don't Ask Don't Tell policy

Don't ask if I'm married / don't tell me if you're a dirty dirty
   "Dirty Girl" or Lolita,

Riot Grrrl, political girl

We can party all night I know this abandoned tree house near . . .

Bring the booze I'll bring my professor-mentor We'll go with the ski bum and the German and the newspaper staff and the bearded one (did you know Americans are still talented enough to restore colonial barns?)

Why, you ask? We want to celebrate, we've pulled off our disguises, we owe it to frank discussions over cold coffee on various and sundry side roads throughout local mid-sized ranges of hills in a mid-size sedan, soulful enough to adore the veil of white all around, desperate enough to want to hide behind it forever,

desperate beauty

we can't do anything with it

It Makes No Difference

Nah, forgot how to write an ode (was at first willing to stay up,
write one for friends scattered,

                           those faces-become-kites

but now, I think the sky thinks they're boring)

Hard to explain to someone who doesn't let words tax them
(that life writing is like being a sofa and hosting a housewarming
party for termites)

Jottings

I wrote the forbidden book.

I threw my smile in the fire.

------

swarm of rats, buzzing of rats
that can only mean a religious conversion –

God's the smell of mice – always on the nose,
          always

Cleaning mice rot from the bookcase –
skinning bats in the eaves. Whistling's
become more fun since they died off

The girl whose stomach rotted is now a stone

Maybe we sit bartering with an angel loudly –
hostile at the hardening of our wings, now shale
or some other form of prison – reeking of seethe –

Rains

So that children will know, I will point to a basic sky.

Samuel Paquin tells me there have been twenty-seven skies, ever
and twenty-seven combs cracked for each.

I feel the sky is broken today like my shiny hillock
on which the minions gather every.

There have been seven million hillocks!

Some of them have crumbled but
   what matters is they never sicken of rain

like the fickle, poetry-reading typico.

Ars Cryotica

True metallurgy: Jupitron Telephone Set,

one end half-brace, half-vibrator, half-friend,

half-vegetable, half-hatchet, half-stuntman,

the other end an end, simply, blunted

crayon type of thing, end.

No one here can spell.

Here, sterile, no one can.

What they *can* do is build Jupitrons nakedly,

contentedly, placidly. Lake Placid dried up.

While we're on locales, Prince Edward Island

is home to convalescent, laser-sutured

stuffed suits with erased histories.

I bought this poem in orange cryovac.

Stay away from the poems in red cryovac,

that's the confessional verse.

Ur-Dissonance

peel the moon peel the moon

syntax of stars falling

heaven peeling away
                    what's behind it

            what being's in it

how does he tend it

with which foregone conclusion does he approach it

how is history kept

who holds the keys to the armoire with the pencil cup
the silver pens

the kind dropped in meadows by runaway poetesses

swish swish wheatfield legs of poets go legs of poets

whisk sunset away whisked away a way a way a way far back

it's so-called night
            so we called it

we named it dark for speechless
was no way to deliver the newborn wonder to our sons our
        daughters

so look look look look up
don't stare you wouldn't want to sit so close, no telling
what'll appear no telling who will charge you for the view,
pretty soon someone will sit shotgun at a toll booth

stroll with a lover share this with them it's free

it's being whisked away by god

too pretty for them he reasons

much too pretty let me hoard it,
let me fill up my loneliness

he has come to admit that he cannot function
without us below, he likes his little circus,

peers at it from behind the moon curtain

listen

a drum roll

the constellations are too clunky

they're being spilled not like diamonds but piss

rusty piss

Fissure

look at the way a girl stares at you

not the way she curves inside

turnstiled flicker sans backlight

issues assuredly blighting the curb

whose feet trample?

never say *ever* on a dock

stop a cistern: to the left a thief

invokes water, uncertain ripplants

but there's a bubble in the plastic

knowe not ask forcefullie

hardy mums – now, laugh!

will your breasts to science

then the sad overture

is there still an uncrossed river

Riverbend

        beneath the vehicle   down the embankment   churning,
Wyoming,   as water might

                    might drill   into an escarpment's
    forméd arches in which a tiny man can   hide

or be   drowned out

even men behind rock can be heard

she stares down   the embankment as
    if there   are men to be heard conversing

Mountains Falling
for___

I can't hear the way the stars think

of the beneath

I can't find the stars (bronze dancers

haggling the late hours into dirt)

Will you transmit – *yes, you're transmitting* – ,

help me understand the sound of a river being crossed

I can't think of anything but the devil's hair

In the Wake of Fallen Mountains

Bond,

Cannon,   Lafayette,

Bondcliff,   Moat,

Lincoln,   Owl's Head,

Flume,

Carrigain,

Lethe,   Osseo,

Tri-Pyramid,

Scar Ridge,

Passaconaway,

. . . .
. . . .
. . . .
. . . .
. . . .
. . . .
. . . .

Fertile evergreens, (plant names, florae, ...) and blindingly
thick.

[things we did there:]

. .
. .
. .
.
.
.

      .

      .

      .

      .

O, requiem.

No more subject matter for Thomas Cole,
                               Frederic Church,
            Thomas Moran,
                     Albert Bierstadt

      &c.,

if they ever came to these parts at all.

Daily the mirror commissions me when it gets the chance.

Tidal lines fanning from my eyes,
                skin complexion like a moving field of wheat,
                    sturdy hue of tawn dotted
    with the small stamens of wheat-bulbs.

So many landscapes
besides mountains.

    ∾

Learn to forget them
        and start tilling your face
     for a sunflower patch

∾

The world is now breathing full with its emptiness −
                 broadened horizons, clearer sightlines.

Up in the once, there. Look, Dogen.

He and I sip coffee outside a tent and scan the not-there.

Do not travel far to other dusty lands, forsaking your own sitting place;
if you cannot find truth where you are you are fucked −

cliffrock, granite, metasiltstones, phyllite, gabbro,

names so full yet empty of truth.

Rock is slick and a killing instrument.

∾

The walk to her home in my sleep, and every night.

The way is empty, yet use will not drain it.

So each night, the empty dreams fill me

and I continue walking, entering the dust.

≈

Portrait With the Entrance of Dusk and Flags Lightly Swimming in Sunset

Attention – Ethan has been lost, apparently

and now life has ruptured –
          a steam hole
pock-marks the happily gray winterside

His is the emptiest church in the world,
where the singers drift about like chrism

Repast sole this hollowness, now the twinge
that never again will I bump into him –

the one into whom something better wandered,
perhaps the gullet otherwise known as night

Procession

my son

digging in the sand

for a toy

I buried there

twenty years ago

he may not

ever avoid

this sun but

the next

sun perhaps

I think of

the sun on

my back

that day

I buried

the toy

and ancient

as the moon

that sun I met

once again

in the sand

speckles

of year-grain

I saw my son

and my toy

and my sun

meet his sun

and worried

of loss

I captured

some sun

in the hole

Still Water

but what is this but what
is

the   fragmentary nature of

a   riverbed   and its   lull

fragmented nature

    of its   spring-fed doxa
spring-fed   doxa   proximity

        father' s farm

father's skiff   father's   dory

        grand found truth in dory acast asea

          writhe sea, undular   sea
    writing   skipping notion

sea

still sea yet river'd sea

still sea yet   anchor'd   harbour'd   and
yet   this is still

more   still   than black
slide

more still than what the urchin knows not

more still than fire turned against us

more still than a name convoluted for ease for
a listener's ease   for but one listener

more murmurs   and murmur   and   back

≈

o forgot-about field

field that says   must rhyme or complete or

the field that it compels water to meet

the field that it compels water to meet

the field that it compels water to meet thusly as a water shall
become that which shall be another water

that   which   was   not   water but   is   by   some compellor

a friend of water

≈

Woe

No God's rain petals –

       puddled, shallow
dreams and drifts

as airy as lambs' eyes

A breeze tosses
      light sentencery

for God loves me

and hid me next to you

The Good

In her eyes, little flecks of good

On her lips, little glistens of good
                    but no good in her hair –

I took it –

absconded –

hid it to tend it,

lost in its blowing wildly,
                    without reason and constant,

unknowable consistency of cold and good

Girl, Night

Night, according to plan.
Girl, according to my dreams –

Girl and night, both the climax
and triumph of the dark, the wind.

Scythe and Dory

out there where there
is the toward:

might the dory gainst
the sea door

knocking swells about
this high

and cutting the surge
gainst one's face

is: that which will cut
the sea surge not

that: that scythe ashore:
for cutting wheat stalks

sulking fields trapped
in fields of lapping in their

slope toward the surge
toward the little dory

Dark Sky and Bulb from Miles Away

grandfather   wounded in war
       carpenter and rabbit-raiser

nightly alone   feeding animals one
 beautiful bulb his only

light the title of this piece means
think when he's thought of receding

and it is unsettling like

 standing in a dark rabbitry
muffled scurrying and occasional

bursts of leaping –
animals frightened by breath   or breeze –

Woe

Such is my little disease –
like a poodle in a meadow
she makes the sky fall out of its joints.

She makes me ask the grass what it's
been through – "What did you go through?"
I crouch. Creaky little melodies –

Can no longer stand the heft
upon which clouds shatter.

Woe

And as I drive off the cobwebs
spun in my eyes obscure road –

one drives toward a direction
and the sun can't hide any more.

"You know, you came like a storm at the wrong time" –

A lingering gentian sun, passing flurries,
passing lightning storms in December, plum-color

assault, December.

Don't stop there, you're leaving out too much.

Just ask the plum color of the passing December
lightning storm, its mingle with flurries and sun,

just ask the moon, it's made its record-setting
x,000th appearance in the children's books

Troubled by Time

Looking at the moon storming in the room.
        No room to storm, no moon to burn.

Reading the rain, sticking to my stories.
        No stories to tack on the wall, no news.

Fading into my former selves. Look at me rust.
        No rain, no rust.

No rust? I'd become invisible . . .

Sparrows

Leering from the eaves
these sad-sacks.

Plunge the scoop in the grain
and dole it out, and repeat –

rabbits and rain, New Hampshire,
no particular October.

Leering from the eaves
these opportunists.

Learn to take sadness
from something other than me.

Reinhardt in Winter
(Stations of the Cross)

Yes, winter is all black.

Frames of black envelop me, yes, each frame
a new frame of black, each black a new frame.

Frames of black sun, sunset sun, trees-at-sunset
sun, (trees-in-sunset sun), awash in sun, in black,

the wash a sunny black, blackened sunniness,
running black sun, trees blackening from dribbling sun,

sun dripping its black sunset on all the trees, leaving
none unretouched with black runniness.

Yes, winter is all black.

End/Again

Trees will back
into essence.

Trees will back
into essence.

Trees will back
into essence;

trees will back
into essence.

～

My mother's home in which, as a child,
she sat perhaps at sun transfixed, dying
beyond a hill, for the first and only time.

First and only time beyond a hill for the
dying, transfixed sun, she sat perhaps
as a child at my mother's home in which

for the first and only time
dying
as a child

beyond a hill
she sat perhaps at sun transfixed.

Errata

*for*__

Down comes the snow in erratic fits.

It is all that comes to mind –
how a droplet of snow
meets the ground only once,

ill-fated union.

I catch myself in the window
with a far-away look, never
more moved to turn into snow.

The Rest

The rest built. Warm
emptiness turned into a
building known as light.

I built my rest to hide from
that which I build to hide from.

That we dreamt atop a warm hill
is of all the kindest dream.

NOTES

The Makeshift:

"Apogee Brevita": Inspired by Alberti, as quoted in Thomas Merton's *Literary Essays.*

"Entries Fitted for Freezing Rain": The title owes partly to a line in untitled poem 46 of Simon Perchik's *Touching the Headstone* (1999).

"Lingerings Near Southern April": The 'blasted oak' was inspired by Charles Burchfield's painting "An April Mood" (1948). Also quotes Li Yu's "Strangers in Saint's Coif" (c. 960).

"The Makeshift" quotes Henry Vaughan's "Quickness."

"The Near-Miss Slides": "The tree must again be a tree" is adapted from a line of Paul Celan's essay, "Edgar Jené and the Dream about the Dream."

"The Root of Everything" quotes Jippensha Ikku's "Hizakurige" (1802).

"The Use of Reinhardt (Stations of the Cross)": The parenthetical refers to the painter's work in the National Gallery, Washington, D.C.

Dead July:

"Gone Music": "Not to take dying so personally" is a line from Franz Wright's "Thoughts of a Solitary Farmhouse," from *The Night World and the Word Night* (1993).

"In the Wake of Fallen Mountains": "Do not travel far to other dusty lands, forsaking your own sitting place; if you cannot find truth where you are..." is adapted from Dogen. "The way is empty, yet use will not drain it" is from Lao-Tzu. The names in the first lines are mountains in northern New Hampshire, arranged on the page according to geographic location.

"Dark Sky and Bulb from Miles Away" is for James Jackson.

"Scythe and Dory": the subject matter was inspired by Andrew Wyeth's dry brush drawings, "Teel's House" and "Teel's Island" (both 1954).

"Reinhardt in Winter (Stations of the Cross)": Again, referring to the painter's work in the National Gallery, Washington, D.C.

[144]

Printed in the United States
1159800001B/262-273